VW Bus

William Burt

MBI

First published in 2003 by Motorbooks International, Galtier Plaza, Suite 200, 380 Jackson Street, St. Paul, MN 55101-3885 USA

Motorbooks International titles are also available at discounts in bulk quantity for industrial or sales-promotional use. For details write to Special Sales Manager at Motorbooks International Wholesalers & Distributors, Galtier Plaza, Suite 200, 380 Jackson Street, St. Paul, MN 55101-3885 USA

Library of Congress Cataloging-in-Publication

Burt, William M.
    Volkswagen bus / by William Burt.
        p. cm. -- (Enthusiast color series)
    ISBN 0-7603-1319-9 (pbk. : alk. paper)
        1. Volkswagen Transporters. I. Title. II. Series.

TL215.V6 B87 2003
629.223'4--dc21

ISBN 0-7603-1319-9

On the front cover: Who could have guessed that the little German Bus was would become so popular in America and around the world, and would become so closely associated with the hippie lifestyle of the 1960s and 1970s?

On the title page: The Bay Window Transporter was extremely popular and was available in many different variations, from pickup trucks to campers.

On the back cover, top: The simple structure of the "Campmobile" contained features such as a sink, icebox, water tank, hanging closet, a dining table, storage areas, and a bench seat that converted to a double bed. **Bottom left:** Like the New Beetle, the New Microbus will be a modern vehicle that resembles its ancestors only in its general appearance. This concept has a 230-horsepower V-6 located in the front. *Volkswagen of America* **Bottom right:** The 23-window Samba model arrived in 1951 and continues to be one of the most coveted of the Transporter models. *Volkswagen of America*

Edited by Peter Bodensteiner
Designed by Design53, St. Paul, Minnesota

Printed in China

Contents

Introduction 7

Chapter 1 **The Survival of Volkswagen and the Birth of the Transporter** 8

Chapter 2 **The Split Window** 20

Chapter 3 **The Bay Window** 38

Chapter 4 **The Wedge and Beyond** 54

Chapter 5 **Community** 74

Index 95

Introduction

The most popular vehicles traveling America's roads today are sport utility vehicles and minivans. In America's auto-driven society, their ample passenger and cargo space are very attractive. For families with kids, small businesses, and heavy travelers, there is no substitute for the minivan. Parents up front, kids in the back, and plenty of space left over for cargo, including a luggage rack on the top when necessary. Since the styling of minivans is never the hottest of topics, the manufacturers primarily market the vehicles' amenities. Built-in televisions, strategically placed cup holders, and collapsible seats are the hot items. The archetypal minivan commercial focuses on the average couple with their 3.2 kids heading off on vacation. Their luggage is neatly packed, their cups are supersecure, and their children are in the back seat with wires in their heads, being mesmerized by cartoons, thus eliminating forever the cries of "how long till we get there." Just once I would like to see a commercial wherein the all-American couple and their 3.2 kids have the "drive to Florida meltdown" that became a tradition in my family.

The SUV and minivan population began to grow in the 1980s, took off in the 1990s and is being refined as the twenty-first century begins. But the truth is that Dodge did not invent the minivan. Further, the concepts that sell these vehicles today were recognized long before the 1980s. Volkswagen first did it in 1950 when they created the Transporter, more commonly called the "Bus."

Perhaps the most wonderful thing about the creation of the Bus was its attitude. The Bus did not have to rely on fancy marketing to be sold. It was what it was. From the buyers, to the press, to the executives and workers at Volkswagen, everyone knew what the Bus was. It was a box on wheels—a vehicle based on the same principle as a shoebox. Early on it was the commercial market that bought Buses, mainly in the effort to rebuild Germany after World War II. Later, the general public grew to love the versatile little vehicle. As a result of its practicality and honesty, the Bus has carved out a place in our culture.

Many first associate the Bus with the hippie culture. Admittedly, it was a Bus-related phenomenon. But for every hippie smoking dope in the back of a Bus, there were dozens of families toting kids and small businesses taking advantage of this reasonably priced vehicle. Before it was over, the Bus would be offered as a two-door pickup, a four-door pickup, a panel van, and a camper. It would make its way from Germany to almost every country on the planet.

More than 50 years after its birth, the Bus lives on. Throughout the country, local clubs keep their machines on the road. Indeed, the purchase of one of these old classics can be a ticket into the entire Bus community. Owners can cruise, camp, restore, and visit to their heart's content. In a world that gets more and more impersonal every day, the Volkswagen community offers not only a classic vehicle, but also a classic lifestyle.

Left: While the entire team of employees at Volkswagen was responsible for the millions of Beetles and Buses, they were led for years by Heinz Nordhoff. Nordhoff took over a struggling company ruined by war and, by combining good managing skills and vision, he made history. *Volkswagen of America*

Chapter 1

The Survival of Volkswagen and the Birth of the Transporter

Before jumping headlong into a discussion of the Volkswagen Transporter, it is best to step back and take a look at the company that created it. Throughout Volkswagen's history, the company has produced some of the most mechanically significant and best-loved vehicles in the world. In the early years, it built its products on a reputation of ingenuity, simplicity, quality, and value, rather than on a flashy image of power and styling. Most recently, the boxy Golf has taken the main role in providing millions with reliable, comfortable, and affordable transportation.

While the designs of the past two decades have not sold as well in the United States as Volkswagen would have liked, they have done incredibly well on the Continent. Perhaps part of the reason is that in the United States, Volkswagen vehicles can have trouble living up the their own legends. Two of the most-loved vehicles in American history were built in the Volkswagen plant

Upper left: Before the Transporter could be a reality, Volkswagen had to rise from the ashes of a devastating war and start over from scratch.

in Wolfsburg, Germany. They were postwar Germany's first mass-marketed automotive designs, the Beetle and the Bus. It is important to remember that both vehicles, and especially the Bus, were created more from necessity than as an expression of styling.

The story of the Volkswagen Bus actually begins with the story of the Beetle.

It is ironic that the Volkswagen Beetle, the world's most popular car, got its start in Germany's Nazi government in the 1930s. The little car that would become deeply loved in North America, Europe, Asia, and South America was originally a dream of none other than Adolf Hitler. The Beetle's design and creation played an important role in the National Socialist Party's program, and it would not have been developed without Hitler's support. It was to be a simple automotive platform that would provide the German people with an inexpensive form of individually owned transportation, and in so doing, produce the most mobile society on earth.

This may not sound like such a radical idea now, but in the early years of the automobile it was. At the time, automobiles were an expensive luxury, especially in Europe.

The United States had leaped ahead of Europe in mass-producing cars with the 1909 introduction of the Model T. Henry Ford's unique concepts of engineering, production, and marketing had put car ownership within the financial reach of a large percentage of Americans and had "mobilized" an entire society. This was what Hitler wanted for Germany. The problem was that during the 1920s and 1930s, Germany was in a state of disaster, bankrupted by the cost of World War I and the war reparations demanded by the Treaty of Versailles. Germans were scrambling for food and shelter and had little time to consider the luxury of an automobile. But Adolf Hitler became chancellor in 1933 with a dream of restoring Germany's status and developing it into the dominant European power. To do this he proposed and supported projects that would promote Germany's advances in science, industry, and technology. Among these projects were the superhighways called autobahns, much like the modern American interstate highways.

Below: This 1935 prototype of the People's Car was tested shortly before World War II. *Volkswagen of America*

Above: During the war, the factory primarily produced military vehicles, including the Kubelwagen and the Schwimmwagen. The Kubelwagen was the German army's equivalent of the jeep (although it was two-wheel drive).

Right: The Schwimmwagen was an amphibious version of the Kubelwagen and could cross small lakes and rivers.

After the war, the factory had to be rebuilt from complete ruin. Not only would Volkswagen succeed in rebuilding it and producing great vehicles, it would also come up with some imaginative manufacturing processes. Long before Japanese companies became famous for streamlined production, the folks at Volkswagen were doing the same. *Volkswagen of America*

In Germany, automobiles were owned by the rich—and there were few rich Germans—so when the autobahns were built, they would have few cars traveling on them. Logic demanded a car affordable to the masses to fill the great new highway system. But with the economy so bad and raw materials so scarce, the car could use few resources. Hence, the concept of a cheap, reliable mode of transportation that anyone could afford—a "People's Car." In 1934, Hitler personally narrowed the design specifications for a little car, specifying a top speed of 80 kilometers per hour (about 50 miles per hour) and fuel consumption of 4 to 5 liters per 100 kilometers (46 to 58

miles per gallon). To top it all off, the car had to cost the buyer less than 1,000 marks.

For the most part, German politicians were much more energetic about the car than the automobile manufacturers. Leaders of the automobile industry did not think the car was possible, mainly for reasons of profitability (or lack thereof). Profit was their motive, and the specifications for the Bug, especially the selling price, made profit very questionable. This industry attitude led the German government to take charge and contract with independent designers.

One of these contractors was a little-known designer named Dr. Ferdinand Porsche, who was

Above and Below: For Volkswagen, the vision of the Bus was a basic vehicle that could be modified to suit a number of commercial uses, especially for small businesses. From farms to cities, the variants of the Bus would become an integral part of the European and American economies. *Volkswagen of America*

struggling to start his new firm. While Porsche gladly accepted the job, he could not move quickly as his "design facility" was the garage at his house. (It is so very appropriate that the Beetle started in a home garage). Although he had only a small operation, by late 1937 Porsche had built three prototypes and had put a total of 100,000 miles on the three. Even with complete designs and working cars, the German auto industry was still not enthusiastic about the little car. Hitler, tired of the private manufacturers' foot-dragging, decided to continue the development of the People's Car through the government.

Although World War II started on September 1, 1939, the first Beetle still rolled off of the assembly line less than a year later, on August 15, 1940. Production continued throughout the war, but with most resources going to defense factories, Beetle production was meager. By late 1944, the war was drawing to a close and the Allied bombing campaign had virtually destroyed the factory and stopped production. Employees had managed to produce more than 600 cars, but most went to Nazi officials. In fact, two of the first Beetle owners were Adolf Hitler and Hermann Goering.

For Germany, World War II ended on May 8, 1945, with the country's infrastructure virtually destroyed and its land to be occupied by American, British, and Russian soldiers. Wisely, the Allies did not punish Germany as they did after World War I, but worked with the Germans to rebuild the country's industry and get the economy working. The Wolfsburg plant, like the

Since Volkswagen proposed the Bus as a good vehicle for both business and recreation, why not combine the two? This factory photo seems to show just that. Note the table base, which happens to be the spare tire. *Volkswagen of America*

When the company did begin selling to the personal market, it focused on both practicality and fun. From the beginning, Volkswagen saw the Bus not only as a business tool, but also as a method of achieving personal freedom with ease. *Volkswagen of America*

By 1950 the Bus was a reality, and production units were beginning to roll off of the assembly line. This 1950 Panelvan was the 10th Bus built by Volkswagen. *Volkswagen of America*

rest of German industry, had been destroyed by Allied bombing. A workforce made up primarily of prisoners of war under British direction quickly began the cleanup and rebuilding, and Wolfsburg was operational by the second half of 1945. Many of the first units produced after the war were made up of whatever parts were available. Some had a saloon body mounted on the chassis of a Kubelwagen, the German army vehicle that greatly resembled the later VW Thing. But the Beetle project, after many years, was finally rolling, and by October 1946 the factory had produced its 10,000th unit.

These efforts were to impact the entire country, as the Beetle would come to play an important role in West Germany's resurrection. It would, in fact, become a friendly ambassador of Germany to just about the whole world.

In 1947, the Beetle was first offered to the public. Also in 1947, the Beetle made its first border crossing, when 56 cars were exported to the Netherlands, and made its first appearance America, brought across the Atlantic by a few returning soldiers who could not part with the little car that they fell in love with on foreign soil. Production in 1948 would ramp up to almost 20,000 cars, and Volkswagen headquarters was moved from Berlin to Wolfsburg. It was also in 1948 that Heinz Nordhoff, a former Opel general manager and a central figure in Volkswagen's success, came to the company.

Another development occurred, almost unseen, during these early years, when the factory was evolving. The Transporter arose, seemingly from nothing.

One day in the factory some employees were pondering how they could more efficiently carry heavy parts around the plant. So they built something—after all, they were surrounded with tools, machinery, and Volkswagen parts. They built their simple, clever little parts shuttle and went back to work, without realizing they had created the foundation for a wondrous vehicle.

Most automotive historians agree that Dutch importer Ben Pon, one of the first in the Volkswagen import/export trade, began the series of events that led from this vehicle to the creation of the Volkswagen Transporter. In 1947, on one of his visits to the Beetle works at Wolfsburg, Pon became intrigued with the odd little homemade factory vehicle. He later drew up a rough sketch of a vehicle he had in mind for the open market. He felt it was right up Volkswagen's alley. It was simple, basically a box with a steering wheel in the front and an engine in the rear, and could be based on the vehicles VW was already building. Pon, a great marketer, felt the postwar world was begging for such a vehicle.

Long before hippies began to paint flowers on them, the VW Bus provided cheap and reliable transportation for light loads. It was the perfect vehicle for small and large businesses. Pon and a few others at Volkswagen envisioned this new platform to be an incredibly handy tool for all types of industries. Businesses from construction firms to flower shops, all short of capital, could take advantage this inexpensive and simple truck-van-bus.

The management at Volkswagen listened to Pon, but the company was having a hard time just making Beetles and felt that starting a new line of vehicle

would not be prudent. Nordhoff, who called it a "box on wheels," was not keen on the idea, but Pon and other advocates persuaded Nordhoff to approve drawing up a serious design. Volkswagen's chief development engineer, Alfred Haesner, worked up two sets of drawings, and the one that Nordhoff liked moved ahead to the prototype phase.

During the prototyping, the Volkswagen engineers learned a good deal. The first prototype was built with the same type of chassis as the Beetle. While this unibody-type chassis was plenty strong for a small four-passenger car, it was not nearly strong enough for a larger unit built to carry a large load. The first prototype failed as the bodied twisted and deformed when introduced to the reality of the road. In the next prototype, a ladder frame with the body welded directly to it solved the problem. Volkswagen engineers were pleased with the vehicle's handling. One of the Transporter's best features is the balance provided by its design. Most other vans and trucks have the engine, as well as the passengers, in front. When the cargo area is empty, the vehicle is nose heavy and light in the back. This can lead to dramatic oversteer, especially in the rain. The Volkswagen design put the engine, transmission, and drivetrain in the rear and the passengers up front, with the cargo carried between the axles. Regardless of the load, empty or full, the balance of the Bus is much more even.

In 1949, eight Bus prototypes were tested. Six took the form of Panelvans, one as a Kombi, and the other as a Microbus. There were no great disasters during testing, and minor improvements were made before production began. These included a different radius on the front body panel, relocation of the pedals, more refined brakes, better seats, and improved heat shielding. The Bus would begin life with the same 25-horsepower engine that powered the Beetle. Volkswagen was still not capable of developing another engine line, a costly proposition. The Bus's performance was not spectacular with the small motor, but the incredibly slow acceleration was helped by the addition of reduction gears in the rear hubs. The first models could only manage a top speed of about 50 miles per hour, but they did sport more than 162 cubic feet of interior cargo space. The no-nonsense design—it could carry its own weight in load—resulted in the employees naming the vehicle "bulli," German for "brawny."

So in 1949, just four years after the end of World War II, Nordhoff announced to the press that the Panelvan would be in production by the end of the year. The initial production rate would be set at 10 units a day, and the Volkswagen team kept its word. The project stayed on schedule, and journalists saw the production Transporter for the first time in November 1949. For viewing, Volkswagen had prepared two Panelvans, one Kombi, and one Microbus.

The fact that any of these vehicles ever got off of the drawing board and onto the road is a small miracle in itself, given the condition of the German company just five years earlier. In modern times, it takes years for the automotive giants to design and bring a new model to market. Volkswagen had rebuilt its factory, begun production of the Beetle, and created, designed, and built the Bus in less then 60 months, all during the difficult years of postwar Germany. During the next 50 years, Volkswagen would become one of the world's automotive giants, but in many ways the company's first five years will always be its most impressive.

The 23-window Samba model arrived in 1951 and continues to be one of the most coveted of the Transporter models. *Volkswagen of America*

It would not be long before Volkswagen was a giant on both land and sea. While millions of its vehicles roamed the roads all over the world, its many ships traveled the oceans, delivering Beetles and Buses. *Volkswagen of America*

Chapter 2

The Split Window

Timing is everything, and the Bus, like the Beetle, had impeccable timing. The strange little vehicle hit the market just when the market needed exactly what it had to offer. Without this timing it might never have made it to production, much less become a sight that is instantly recognized all over the planet.

Ben Pon had been right about the vehicle's potential. The Bus was so versatile that for decades it would keep up with the times, always being able to fit a niche and opening up markets all over the world. Because of Europe's need for work vehicles, Volkswagen decided that the Panelvan would be the first model to go into production, and the first units began coming off the assembly line in early 1950. Production started slowly. Seven units were produced in January, and only three in February. Then the factory began to get it rolling, producing more than 300 units in March and April.

Above: When the Bus made its public appearance, the world had never seen anything like it. The vehicle's look, especially from the front, was about as pleasant as an automotive expression can get. It seemed to have big round eyes and a large sharp nose, and it wore a perpetual smile.

Buyers loved their new Panelvans. The ladder frame construction made it capable of carrying quite large loads; in fact, the first Buses could carry 750 kilograms (1,654 pounds) of cargo or passengers. Its bench seats could carry up to eight people, or the rear seats could be easily removed to transform it into a cargo carrier.

Much like the early Beetles, the first Buses were built with what was on hand. It was still only five years after the war's end, and the factory did not have enough resources to get fancy. To simplify production the first Buses used as many existing parts as possible, including Beetle engines and axles. Like the Beetle, the first Bus engine had a displacement of 1,131 cc. The cylinder bore on the four-cylinder air-cooled engine was 75 millimeters (2.95 inches) and the stroke was 64 millimeters (2.52 inches). It produced about 25 horsepower at 3,300 rpm. The compression was held to a mild 5.8 to 1 because of the likelihood of getting poor-quality fuel in Germany after the war. Fuel capacity was 8.8 gallons. By today's standards the Bus was very, very slow. On a good day it could run at 55 miles per

hour, but with a load aboard it could take more than two minutes to achieve that speed. The electrical system was six-volt, quite popular at the time. Autos in the 1940s and 1950s did not have nearly the appetite for electricity that modern automobiles have, but six-volt systems are not nearly as powerful as 12-volt systems, so cold starting would occasionally be a problem for Volkswagen owners. The Bus's independent rear suspension consisted of parallel trailing arms, torsion bars for spring, and shock absorbers. The front suspension also received its spring from torsion bars and dampening from shocks. Unlike the Beetle, the

Below and top right: The first model slated for production would be the Panelvan. This version would firmly entrench itself in the commercial market, while the factory began gearing up the designs for personal transportation. Only five years had passed since the war's end, and the Panelvan was a great help in rebuilding Europe. *Volkswagen of America*

Bus would begin life with hydraulically activated brakes, with drums and shoes on all four wheels.

Torsion bar suspensions have been around for years and can be found on vehicle types ranging from Volkswagen Beetles and Buses to old Dodge Chargers to military tanks (which still use them). Instead of using a coil or leaf spring, the most common spring devices on modern autos, these vehicles use heavy steel bars, which run from side to side on both the front and

In the early years, cleaners offered one of the biggest markets for the Panelvan. The large cargo area and the easy access of the side "barn doors" made the vehicle a great choice for any business engaged in pickup and delivery. *Volkswagen of America*

rear suspension. The bars are twisted, or "loaded," and an arm is attached to each end. The bar's tendency to want to "untwist" itself provides the spring.

The Buses that came off of the assembly line in the first few years were very basic vehicles by today's standards. All of the components were an exercise in simplicity. Headlights, running lights, mirrors, door handles, and wipers were of a very basic but functional design. Engine-cooling vents were simply cut and pressed out of the body panel, and windows were flat glass. Inside the Bus, things were just as Spartan. Seats were simple benches. Instrumentation was limited to a

speedometer. Door panels were little more than cloth-covered fiberboard, and the floor was covered with rubber mats. Vehicles on the road in the early 1950s were much more basic than they are today, and it was common for items such as oil filters and heaters to be offered as options. Compared to its competition in the commercial market, the Bus was a breath of fresh air. The commercial vehicles available to businesses at the time were typically slow, noisy, and far less refined than even the basic Panelvan. Even with its small motor, the Bus performed well in its role as a pack mule. Production in the first years centered on the Panelvan model, which was the base vehicle built for commercial use. Second in production for 1950 was the Kombi variant, which was basically a Panelvan with side windows, designed as a people mover. Although the Kombi had two rear bench seats for passengers, they could easily be removed and the Kombi could haul cargo like a Panelvan. Third in early production was the more refined Microbus. When 1950 ended, the factory had produced 8,000 Buses. The output consisted of 5,662 Panelvans, 1,142 Microbuses, and 1,254 Kombis. Additionally one Pickup variant sneaked through the assembly line.

At Volkswagen, expectations for the Transporter were high. As more and more Transporters hit the streets, the press, the commercial market, and the private market all showed great enthusiasm for Volkswagen's new creation. Few engineering changes were made before entering into the second year of production, and those that were made were of minor

suspension changes and the introduction of a small rear window. The front emblem was also changed from aluminum to steel. As with the Beetle, the company was not prone to make great changes to the vehicle at one time, but instead to slowly refine the vehicle with a few changes year to year.

The Bus was a success, and Volkswagen knew it. From 1950 to 1964, annual sales of the vehicle would increase without a major redesign. It would have been easy to modify it to the point that what sold the vehicle in the first place would be gone. Even without Detroit-style new-model hoopla, admirers found excitement in new Volkswagens.

The big news in 1951 was the introduction of the Microbus Deluxe, or the Samba. By the end of the year, the factory would only turn out 269 of the model, but its image was impressive. To this day, the Samba is one of the most coveted of all of the Buses. Like the Kombi, the Samba was built more for transporting

continued on page 26

Left: Not only could the Bus be used for carrying cargo and people, it could also be a traveling office. This enterprising accountant was always sure he would have office space when auditing his clients' records. *Volkswagen of America*

On the next two pages: The little air-cooled engine that powered the Bus started with a modest 25 horsepower. Over the next three decades the vehicle would keep this engine, although frequent upgrades and increased displacement would more than double the power output.

While it was not produced in volume until 1952, the Pickup variant of the Transporter became a big seller for Volkswagen. By 1960, the annual sales of the Pickup model were exceeded only by the Panelvan.

continued from page 23

people than cargo. Snazzy two-color paint schemes and lots of chrome gave the vehicle a great look, and the vehicle's 23 windows and rollback roof gave passengers great visibility. From 1950 to 1955, Microbus and Samba buyers could choose from three paint schemes: brown beige over light beige, stone gray over stone gray, or chestnut brown over sealing wax red. While essentially the same mechani-cally as the early commercial Panelvans, the Samba gave the appearance of being quite different. Instead of a drab appearance, the Samba was vibrant; just looking at it seemed to bring on visions of good times. While many manufacturers were leaning toward producing sleek, mean-looking machines, Volkswagen wasn't. The Samba was about as aggressive as Santa Claus.

Above: The bed of the Pickup featured sides and a tailgate that folded down, allowing conversion to a flatbed. This made for easier loading, and provided for hauling large, bulky items.

Left: The first Buses featured a unique front windshield setup, which allowed the windows to be opened at the bottom to allow airflow to the cab. While this did allow for air circulation, it also gave dust and other debris an almost direct path to the driver's eyes.

The redesign of 1965 included a larger rear window, which meant two of the 23 windows would be lost on the Samba. This turned the 23 Window into the 21 Window. The change did not detract from the vehicle's unique good looks.

When production ended in 1951, the figures were again encouraging. Production had increased from 8,000 total units in 1950 to 12,000 in 1951. Again, the highest production model was the basic Panelvan, with 6,000 produced. Sales of the Kombi and Microbus models both more than doubled from the previous year. And once again, one Pickup was produced. Along with the Samba, another new model appeared in 1951, when the factory produced 36 ambulances on the Bus platform. While the ambulance would never be a huge seller, its sales would hold strong for many years, peaking at over 2,000 units in 1973.

After two years of production, filled with the pressure that accompanies all new models, the company began to analyze the success of the Bus. New models enter the market deep in a financial hole, due to the investment in engineering, testing, tooling up production, and marketing before the first unit can be sold. Volkswagen had minimized these startup costs for the Bus by using many parts from the Beetle, but it had still been a big risk, given the shortage of resources.

Above: With the addition of a rollback roof, the Samba seemed to be as much air as metal, allowing passengers to travel with as good a view as in any vehicle ever made. The side "barn doors" made passenger entry a bit easier.

Left: While comfortable and functional, the interior of the Bus was quite basic. The driver was given a steering wheel, a speedometer, and pedals, and that was about it.

For the VW Bus, the news was good. Production rose again in 1952, with output soaring to 21,665 total units. A very encouraging sign for the factory was the heavy sales growth in every variant of the Bus. The cargo market for the functional Panelvan continued to be strong, with the factory producing 9,353 of them, representing 43 percent of total Bus production for that year.

The passenger area of the Samba was just as basic, but nonetheless comfortable for the times. The rear seats could be easily removed to haul bulky cargo.

Those in search of functionality were also offered a second choice in 1952. The factory had perfected the Pickup model and by year's end would produce 1,600 units. While the Pickup was a variant of the Panelvan platform, it was a more intensive engineering conversion than the Ambulance, Samba, or Kombi. The Pickup was also well received by press and public. Its bed offered four square meters (43 square feet) of cargo capacity. Volkswagen was on a roll. It seemed that no matter what skin covered the Bus, it was a sales success. The Pickup, like the other models, turned out to be very popular with many buyers, especially light construction and small businesses.

Added to the strong sales of the Pickup line was the Ambulance market, which grew by more than 12 times, with 481 leaving the factory in 1952. Moving healthy people was booming as well, with the growth of the more "passenger-oriented" Buses. Microbus

production rose to 4,052 units. Kombi popularity also continued to rise, with 5,031 coming off of the assembly line, and the new Samba was gaining speed, with 1,142 being produced in its second year.

There were again no major engineering changes to the Bus in 1952. None of the few minor changes that were made heavily affected any of the operating systems. This put the total yearly production of Buses at 21,000 units. The VW Bus had grown from an offhand idea to be an important revenue producer for the company, but success was to have it own problems—demand was outpacing Volkswagen's manufacturing capacity. It was time to think about more production capacity, so the factory cranked out as many Buses as it could and began to plan for the future.

The first major change to the Bus would come in 1953, with the introduction of the 30-horsepower engine. The new motor, not introduced until

The Single Cab Pickup was followed in 1958 by the Double Cab Pickup. It combined the benefits of the Pickup with space for extra passengers or a fair amount of luggage.

The rear area meant that a bit of bed space was lost, but for those who drove their Pickups daily, or had children, it was a good trade.

December, had a displacement of 1,192 cc versus the 1,131 cc of the original engine. The increase in displacement was achieved by increasing the cylinder bore from 75 to 77 millimeters (2.95 to 3.03 inches). While 30 horsepower cannot be considered very powerful (other engines could make that much power with one cylinder), buyers greatly appreciated the 5-horsepower increase, which represented a 20 percent increase from the 25-horsepower model. The other significant change in 1953 was the addition of a rear bumper to the Panelvan.

Production in 1953 continued to climb, growing from 21,665 total units to 28,417. Panelvan, Microbus, Samba, and Kombi production were all up from the previous year. The big gainer in 1953 was the Pickup model. Production rose from 1,606 to 5,741 units, a whopping 257 percent. In only its second year, the Pickup was the second-highest model in sales,

Above: As Campers became more popular, they became fancier. Cabinets were an integral part of the conversion, allowing for items to be securely stored while traveling. The early Campers were classics and had the charm of an old wicker picnic basket.

The rear of the Camper was used for storage while traveling, converting to a bed once the travelers had arrived.

surpassed only by the Panelvan. Again, it seemed that regardless of what Volkswagen did with it, the Bus had what the market wanted. In late 1954 the 100,000th Bus was completed. At the time, Bus production was running at about 80 units per day, but the capacity problem was becoming more severe. The Bus had shown its worth to Volkswagen many times over and

With a bit of extra headroom provided by the roof modifications, it was possible for a person to stand up while dressing or cooking in the Camper.

there were few skeptics left. The company would reward it with a grand investment. On March 1, 1955, construction began on a dedicated Bus factory in Stocken, a suburb of Hanover, Germany.

The move to Hanover was accompanied by a few more design changes. The area above the windshield was redesigned. The new one had a more pronounced peak instead of a simple water channel. Below this "peak" were "air pickups" for interior ventilation. In 1953, the Bus had gotten a bit more power, so by 1955 the factory would work to help it slow down and steer a bit better. The front brakes went from single-cylinder actuation to dual cylinders in 1955, and the brake master cylinder, the front and rear wheel cylinders, and the front brake shoes were increased in size. As a result, the front braking surface increased from about 700 square centimeters to 836 square centimeters. The factory also added a steering damper to improve the steering action and feedback to the driver.

Meanwhile, it didn't take long for Volkswagen to get the new Bus factory rolling. In less than two years, the factory went from paper to production. By 1956, units produced at Hanover were available. The factory's 5,000 employees would soon be pumping out 200 Buses a day. When 1957 came to a close, the Bus had completed eight years of production. The

The Camper conversions started with the Split Window, and they are still a Volkswagen mainstay and popular to this day. Companies such as Westfalia would take the Transporter from Volkswagen and convert it for use as a weekend getaway vehicle.

In 1966, the electrical system of the Bus was converted from six to 12 volts. The extra power was a welcome addition, especially when cranking up on very cold mornings.

first four years had been good for Volkswagen, with the vehicle becoming firmly entrenched in the European market, and the next four had been stupendous. Throughout the mid-1950s, growth was seen again in all the model ranges. Panelvan production rose to 30,000 in 1957. In the same period, the Microbus grew to 17,000. The Samba rose to 3,500 and the Kombi to 23,000. The Pickup model was possibly the biggest surprise, with production soaring to 16,450 in 1957. Combining all models, the Bus sold slightly more than 8,000 units in 1950, 40,000 in 1954 and 92,000 in 1957.

Volkswagen had great confidence in its little workhorse by 1958, and it showed that confidence by introducing a new model. As Pickups had become increasingly popular in the late 1950s, the company decided to expand that line. The factory once again did a little drawing, engineering, and modifying and

the result was the introduction of the Crewcab. It is interesting that among the hottest-selling items at the beginning of the twenty-first century are extended cab and four-door pickups. Many not familiar with Volkswagen think of these vehicles as a recent phenomenon, but Volkswagen was there about 40 years before most of the current manufacturers. The Crewcab offered then what it does now—a functional truck with a bit more interior than a standard model.

Another major program introduced by the factory in 1958 was the reconditioning program. Customers who had worn out an engine could get a refurbished replacement engine from Volkswagen for about half the price of a new factory engine. It allowed loyal customers to keep their older Buses rolling without a huge bill, again a big advantage for small businesses. No major changes were made for 1959, but sales again increased from 101,000 units in 1958 to 121,000 in 1959.

The 1960s began with good news for all who were looking to buy a new Bus. In 1960, the box on wheels would again gain a bit more power, when the 34-horsepower engine became available. Most of the power increase was achieved by increasing the compression of the existing motor from 6.6:1 to 7.0:1. Another practical option that became available in 1961 was the high-roof model, especially welcomed by businesses that had to deal with bulky or lightweight cargo. The German post office, as an example, used many high-roof Buses. During the 1962 production year, the one-millionth Bus was produced, and sales were still climbing. They moved from just under 140,000 units in 1960 to 152,000 in 1961, and on to almost 166,000 in 1962. In 1963, the number would again rise, almost reaching the 175,000 mark. The simple box on wheels seemed to have no limit when it came to sales growth.

Relatively major changes were in store for the Bus in 1963, and the big change once again centered on power. In 1963, the American market could get a Bus with the newer 1,500 cc engine. The 1,500 would also take over the European market, and by 1965 the 1,200 had disappeared from the Bus line. The 1,500 (actually 1,493 cc) was rated at 42 horsepower at 3,800 rpm. The engine had a bore of 83 millimeters (3.27 inches) x 69 millimeters (2.72 inches) and 7.5:1 compression. The new, more powerful engine improved performance and made it possible for the cargo rating to go from 750 kilograms (1,654 pounds) to 1,000 kilograms (2,205 pounds).

Passenger heating was made better and safer in 1963, when the heater boxes were replaced with heat exchangers. The brake system became safer when a dual master cylinder allowed the front and rear brake lines to operate separately.

By 1964, Volkswagen had two of the hottest-selling vehicles in the world, and it owned one of the biggest fleets on the oceans, exporting cars and Buses everywhere. The Bus was extremely popular in its native Germany and was popping up all over the globe, with America becoming one of its hottest markets. The Split Window was popular with the 1960s counterculture as well as with families and those who just wanted something a bit different. In late 1965, the 1,500 got bigger valves, which allowed the little motor to pick up a couple more horsepower. The rear window and tailgate became wider, so wide in fact that two of the 23 windows were dropped from the Microbus Deluxe. The rear quarter-windows were eliminated, due to lack of room with the introduction of a new tailgate, so the "23 Window" Bus became the "21 Window." A 12-volt electrical system was introduced in 1966, greatly increasing the chance that a bus would crank on the coldest of mornings.

And although the first generation of Transporters was on the way out, the factory was still making improvements to a chassis that was now getting long in the tooth. Sales of all models had grown steadily across the board since the late 1950s, and total production had topped the 100,000-unit mark in 1958. By 1964, Split Window sales peaked at 188,000 total units. In 1965, for the first time, sales of all models, with exception of the Ambulance, declined from the previous year, for a total decrease of 12,000 units. Total production dropped again the following year—it was time for a change.

Engineers and draftsmen at Volkswagen were busy coming up with the next-generation Bus. They had to be careful. More than 1.8 million Split Windows had been sold, and the Bus was clearly loved by buyers. Volkswagen was in the unenviable position of having to change a very successful product, and it would be difficult to improve safety, comfort, and performance without changing the vehicle to the extent that buyers were offended. If you discount the opinions of the ultrapurist Bus collectors, Volkswagen succeeded. The last Split Window Bus came off of the production line in August 1967, ending production of a vehicle that had greatly improved Volkswagen's image and bottom line. The next Bus coming off the line would be a Bay, rather than a Split.

By the mid-1960s, the factory was working on a replacement for the Split Window, and by 1967 the days of the Split Window were over. While later generations of the vehicle would be more powerful, more comfortable, and safer, the original design was the greatest Transporter ever. Had it not been successful, the other generations would never have existed. Over a half-century has passed since the smiling Bus made its appearance, and to this day few vehicles will produce stares like a finely restored Split Window.

Chapter 3

The Bay Window

The first-generation Bus had lasted 16 years without a major redesign. After its 1950 introduction, the Split Window had been received by both commercial and private customers with great enthusiasm. It can be argued that Volkswagen's creation, for the times, was the most versatile, imaginative vehicle ever built. Look at what it offered. Large families could fit in all of the kids and a bit of luggage without being cramped. The "halfway" outdoorsmen could drive to a campsite and have a very comfortable abode. Small businesses could use the Bus as an inexpensive delivery vehicle. With the many variations available, the Bus was a flexible business tool that could fill many roles. In the 1990s, minivans and four-door pickup trucks became popular, causing the press and public to marvel at the usefulness of the "new" designs, with few remembering that Volkswagen offered both in the 1950s.

Above: The Bay Window had a completely different look from the Split Window. While it may have lost some of its "classic" look, it was plainer in a pleasing way.

The company's marketing goal was to keep the positive features that made the Split Window such a success, while refining or redesigning any of its weak points. It was much easier said than done. Products with a cult following may be easier to sell, but Rule Number One is "Don't offend the cult." Just as the loyalty of its members equates to sales, their anger equates to boycotts. The Bus had enjoyed a strange success in the United States, where "better" usually means faster, bigger, and fancier. The Bus often sold in America precisely because it was different. Its lack of refinement and slow speed were accepted fondly. So the engineers faced a daunting task: to make the new vehicle the same as the first generation in some ways, but different in others. It was a time of great change for Volkswagen, not only because of the new Bus, but also because of the introduction of a new Beetle. This was the environment in 1967, when the second generation Bus was introduced.

While the design philosophy remained the same overall—a box on wheels—the new version of the Bus was drawn on a blank sheet. The new body would in

In 1968, the Bay Window rolled onto the scene. When the new vehicle made its appearance, some discounted it because of a perceived loss of personality, but this was a short-sighted attitude. The Bay Window was an excellent vehicle, and the buying public would agree.

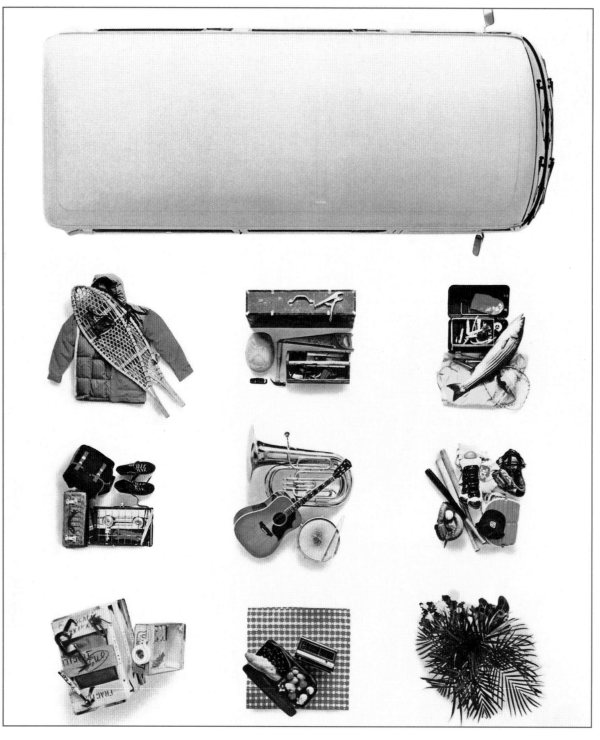

no way be mistaken for the old one. Perhaps the most noticeable change to the body was to the front. The oncoming view of the new Type 2 would be markedly different, and would be one of the major gripes for many early Bus loyalists. The most noticeable difference to the bow of the Bus was the large, curved, single piece of glass that replaced the split front windshield. It greatly increased visibility, as it eliminated the center bar, stylish but a visual obstruction. The new glass was 25 percent larger, which also added to the view. Its smooth radius shape would be responsible for the new vehicle's nickname, the "Bay Window."

Opposite: Volkswagen did an excellent job of advertising the benefits of the new Type 2. Flexibility was a strong selling point, and it worked. *Volkswagen of America*

Below: The Bay Window took over where the Split Window stopped. It was immediately recognized as a versatile workhorse that could get you to work during the week and get you to relaxation on the weekend.

Also gone from the front body panel was the "hawk's beak" relief, pressed in the sheet metal front, that ran from below the windshield to just above the front bumper. Instead of the "hawk's beak," a rectangular shape with rounded corners rose from the front sheet metal. Turn signal indicators went from a round design above the headlights to rectangular units mounted below the headlights. Headlight mounting points were recessed instead of raised, and a vent area with vertical slits was added just under the windshield. The result was a much "cleaner," more efficient look, with a lot less going on in the front. Although it was a cleaner design, there was no doubt the vehicle lost a bit of personality. But much more had changed besides the front.

At a glance, the sides of the new vehicle were similar, but a closer inspection showed a few significant differences. The front doors, which kept the same shape, were a bit wider and had recessed hinges, which provided both a cleaner look and cleaner airflow

Throughout its life, the Bay Window would be blessed with more and more power. While it was still slow, it was not as painfully slow as the Split Window. With its greater horsepower, the Bay Window did not have reduction gears.

around the body. The Bus was never the most aerodynamic of vehicles, but with its tendency to be chronically underpowered, every bit helped. The sliding side door also became a full-time feature, replacing the old "barn door" design and eliminating the vertical line where the two doors met. The new door allowed easier loading and unloading in tight spaces, a big improvement for businesses that used the Bus as a delivery vehicle.

The slotted engine air intakes were also modified and moved. While they had been refined throughout the life of the Split Window, they had remained essentially the same, pressed into the sheet metal under the side windows toward the rear. The new air intakes were moved as far up and back as possible. On the new Type 2 they would reside behind the rear side window in a crescent-shaped housing. The new housing had some positive relief, so that at speed there would be a slight ram-air effect. Each side now sported three large windows instead of three or four smaller ones. The new body design brought on perhaps the most painful departure from the Split Window, the end of the 21-Window variants. With the top of the Bay Window being a bit flatter than the Split Window, the new sheet-metal configuration meant it would no longer be possible to insert the curved upper windows into the body.

Not only was the new body different aesthetically, it also grew physically. Overall, the new body was 4–5 inches longer (100–125 millimeters) than its predecessor. The new Bus was also heavier than its predecessor, weighing in at 2,590 pounds (1,175 kilograms), compared to 2,015 pounds (914 kilograms) for the Split Window. The new interior was also a step up. Although it was still more functional than fancy, the new Bus would sport a padded dash and a fuel gauge. Passenger comfort was also addressed with the introduction of better seats and a better ventilation system. Interior options varied widely between models, but all were a bit more refined. The bigger body and bigger windows also meant that driver visibility was improved in all directions. To push the extra weight, the new Bus would also have more power, accomplished by increasing the engine's displacement to 1,584 cc and increasing the compression ratio to 7.5:1, which allowed the new engine to put out 50 horsepower. While the new engine did not turn the Bus into a rocket ship, every bit of power helped, and with 50 horsepower the updated Bus had twice the power of the first models. With the increased power and a bit of change in the gearing, the Bay Window would not require reduction gears to aid in low-speed acceleration. This also saved weight and eliminated an entire mechanical system from the vehicle. Power was put to the wheels through a four-speed manual transmission. The suspension remained basically the same, with spring still being achieved through torsion bars, while the brakes received some minor updates. Although the second generation was introduced with drum brakes on all four wheels, the brakes were activated by a dual-circuit master cylinder and line setup. This meant that the front and rear brakes were activated by separate hydraulic systems, safer because one system would keep its integrity if the other failed.

The results of all of the changes were quite positive. Performance for the new Bus was a maximum speed of about 70 miles per hour, with acceleration to 50 miles per hour taking about 23 seconds. While most cars had much better acceleration and top speed, the Bus was not a car; and when compared to its predecessors, the new Type 2 showed a dramatic performance increase. One very positive performance statistic for

Moving large numbers of passengers was still a primary function of the Bus. Passengers still rode on bench seats, which could be easily removed to transport cargo.

the new model was its ability to cover about 25 miles on one gallon of gasoline, a figure that was not as important in the cheap gas years of the 1960s but would become much more of a factor in the 1970s.

From the beginning of production, the Bay Window platform was available in all the standard Transporter configurations—Kombi, Microbus, Microbus Deluxe, Panelvan, Single Cab Pickup, and Double Cab Pickup. The Bay Window showed up just in time to celebrate another milestone production figure. In 1968, the two millionth Transporter rolled off of the assembly line.

The celebration at Volkswagen would be short-lived, marred by the April 1968 death of Heinz Nordhoff, the man who had been so instrumental in the growth and success of Volkswagen. Nordhoff had led the company from 1948 to 1968, and made it one of the most successful automotive companies in the world. But with vehicles as popular as the Beetle and the Bus, he left the company in a great condition. In the manner of great managers, Nordhoff had assembled an organization that could continue to thrive in his absence. The managers who succeeded Nordhoff at Volkswagen knew that the show must go on.

As the sales numbers began to come in, it was obvious that the new Bus was getting off to a great start. In 1968, the first full year of production, the new Type 2 sold 228,000 units, a sales record. The total sales figure was split between 51,000 Panelvans, 64,000 Microbuses, 68,000 Kombis, 31,000 Pickups, 12,000

Below and opposite: The Pickup model would be continued on the Bay chassis and would remain a strong seller. In fact, this Pickup was made in Brazil in 1986, long after production was ended in Europe. By importing the Pickup in pieces and assembling it on arrival, the buyer could get around the import laws and still enjoy an air-cooled classic in America.

Double Cabs, and 1,200 Ambulances. All of the models were selling very well, so the designers could breathe a bit easier. The new design was well received and, more importantly, it was profitable. Virtually no changes were ordered for the 1969 line, and sales increased again. While some loyalists mumbled about missing the Split Window and contended that it had more character than the new model, the Volkswagen sales force was very happy. In 1970, the factory churned out almost 258,000 Buses, another production record for the Bus, and for the first time the quarter-million mark had been reached. Volkswagen sold almost 78,000 Kombis alone. The new design may have lost a bit of character, but the Bay Window was a much more refined vehicle, and buyers knew it.

As the 1970s began, the factory again started the methodical process of refining the new Bus, addressing both performance and safety. One of the biggest changes came in late 1970, when the Bus finally dropped the front drum brakes in favor of disc brakes. In the ever-continuing quest for more power, the relatively new 1,600 got twin-port cylinder heads, which helped performance. The next year, in late 1971, power once again increased with the introduction of a new engine, the 1,700. The 1,700 (actually 1,679)-cc engine produced 65 horsepower at 4,800 rpm. The 1,700 engine was an option in the European market but was standard equipment in the United States. The air intakes on the side of the Bus were increased in size to help cool the new power plant. The heavy sales figures,

Camper conversions were a hot seller, and Volkswagen knew it. The company made them a mainstay of its advertising campaign.

largely due to the export markets, meant that production milestones were coming faster and faster. In 1971, the three-millionth Bus was built. The bigger engines hit the streets in force in 1972, and for the third straight year the factory would sell a quarter-million Buses.

For the rest of the 1970s, there would be no more major modifications of the Bay Window, with the exception of ever-increasing displacement engines. Most changes were simply refinements, such as the option of a three-speed automatic transmission for Buses with the 1,700-cc engine, or moving the front turn signals from above the bumper to well above

the headlights. The latter was seen as a safety issue, as the lower position made them much more difficult for approaching traffic to see. In 1974, the 1,800-cc engine was introduced. Instead of standard carburetion, this unit came with Bosch Jetronic fuel injection, a move that helped the Bus comply with emission laws. A three-point seatbelt for the driver became standard in 1974, as did halogen headlights. Displacement went up again in 1976 when the two-liter engine became available. The new 1,970-cc engine produced about 70 horsepower. During this time, Volkswagen engineers had to worry not only about finding more power, but

continued on page 51

Above: The driver's appointments had become much more comfortable with the Bay Window. The Bay featured more comfortable seats, better seatbelts, more gauges, and a padded dash.

On the next two pages: Contained within the simple structure of the "Campmobile" were features that included a sink, icebox, water tank, ceiling lamp, hanging closet, storage areas, dining table, and a bench seat that converted to a double bed. The deluxe version also included a two-burner stove and a 12-volt refrigerator. Campers became more and more complex during the Bay years. It was possibly the ultimate combination of nimble daily driver and weekend camper.

Above: With the addition of a custom tent, the vehicle could quickly become a spacious home away from home.

Opposite: With a little bit of paint and style, the Bus could be tailored to anyone's individuality. Take Der Kruzenwagen, for example.

continued from page 46

also about doing it with fewer emissions. As the Bus was exported to so many different countries, the factory had to meet a number of different requirements.

In 1977, Bus number 4,500,000 rolled off the assembly line, and while sales were still strong, they were declining. The biggest year for the Bay Window had been 1972, when the factory produced 259,000 units. Sales had then begun a steady decline, and by 1978 production was back to about 150,000 units. All of the models, from Microbuses to Pickups, were

down, largely because of the competition that had arisen. By the late 1970s, Ford, Dodge, and Chevrolet had made great strides in van production, and American and Japanese small trucks had taken the wind out of the Single Cab and Double Cab sales.

The Bay Window had been around for a dozen years, and again it was time for a change, but by this time there was little more to be done to it. There were not really any changes that would make it better in its class. (Actually, there were no other vehicles in its class.) American vans of the time were a far cry from the Bus, and to compete with them, the vehicle would have to be totally reengineered. U.S. vans usually sported a powerful V-8 mounted in the front, providing good acceleration and plenty of towing power. The interior choices ranged from basic service vans to the living room on the road, complete with captain's chairs, a table, shag carpeting, lots of wood trim, power to tow, and cold, cold air conditioning. There was no way the Volkswagen engineers could or would take the Bay Window down that road. The luxury Microbus was the fanciest and most comfort-able mode Volkswagen had to offer, and it was a far cry from the Dodges, Chevys, and Fords. Volkswagen could see the writing on the wall, and there were few changes to the Bay Window in the vehicle's last two years.

Another era ended in 1979, as the Bay Window was discontinued. It had been an incredible run. From 1967 to 1979, the Bay Window sold almost 2-1/2 million units. For only the second time in 27 years, the Volkswagen engineers would completely redesign the Bus.

The end of the Bay Window came in 1979. Although the Bay Window had a shorter production run than the Split Window, it sold more units. It would be the end of the heyday of the air-cooled Buses. The vehicles that would follow would be more comfortable and more efficient, but when the Bay Window died, the wonderful vehicle that Arlo Guthrie filled with that pile of garbage was gone.

The soundness of the Bay Window design and construction allowed for years of use with very little maintenance or attention. Many still give owners great loyalty for very little attention in return.

Chapter 4

The Wedge and Beyond

For many Volkswagen enthusiasts, the end of Bay Window production was the end of the glory years for the Bus. For only the second time since its inception in 1950, a whopping 30 years, the Bus was radically redesigned. The Bay Window would give way to the third-generation Bus, soon to be tagged "the Wedge." As radical as the changes were between the first and second generations, the next generation of the Bus would make them pale in comparison. It was a move that carried a substantial risk for Volkswagen, facing the same buyer loyalty issues that arose with discontinuing the Split Window. Added to this was the fact that it was a tenuous time for many industries in both Europe and America. The world was changing quickly, and it was having great impact on all automotive manufacturers.

Above: The Wedge was a great departure from the previous two models of the Transporter in more than body shape. Refinements had been made to just about every part of the vehicle—except the engine. The Wedge began production with an air-cooled engine, but because of the increased weight, it was as slow as the Bay Windows. *Volkswagen of America*

The successor to the Beetle in Europe and America would be the Golf, or, as it was known in America, the Rabbit. The car would go on to become one of the most popular cars ever sold in Europe, but in America it did not produce the results that the Beetle did. The front-engine design and more conventional body made this Volkswagen look like many other cars, so there was no mystique factor. Sure, Volkswagens were known for quality, but now they had much more competition in their class of cars, like the Japanese imports. Another problem with the Rabbit was that American drivers, unfamiliar with diesel power in a small car, would see a diesel-powered Rabbit smoke a bit during acceleration and believe the new Volkswagens had engine problems. The result was that many loyal Volkswagen buyers stayed with their old air-cooled models instead of moving up to the Rabbit or its sportier cousin, the Scirocco. Others bought cars built by Toyota, Datsun, and Honda. The van market was also much more competitive. The posh vans offered by the big three American car companies were much more comfortable and powerful than the Bus. In the commercial market, buyers were looking for more power and cargo capacity, and in this area VW Buses could not compete with the V-8 vans.

So, as the world changed, Volkswagen had no choice but to change with it. It would be a very dramatic change and would produce mixed results. When the press and public finally got a good look at the new Bus, it was clear just how radical the Volkswagen designers had been. Body transitions had much tighter radiuses, and this gave the vehicle a pronounced angular look, replacing the gentle curves along the edges of the Bay Window. The vertical front, which had been common to both the first- and second-generation models, was gone, replaced by a raked windshield. For the third

time, the Bus was nicknamed by look of its front. The third generation became "The Wedge." It had much more of a box shape than the earlier designs, both of which more nearly resembled a bread loaf.

The new body would be 15 feet long, 5.9 feet wide, and 6.4 feet tall. The tires would ride on a 96.9-inch wheelbase with a 61.8-inch track. This meant that the body was longer, wider, and taller, and it had a longer wheelbase than the Bay Window. Despite the increased size, the turning radius of the new Bus was actually tighter, making it more maneuverable in tight quarters than either the Bay Window or the Split Window. The Wedge was heavier than its predecessor, weighing in at 1,985 kilograms (4,377 pounds). The chassis was also

Beginning in 1979, Volkswagen would prepare its customers for a new shape and educate them on the benefits of the new design to come in 1980. The transporter went from the Split Window to the Bay Window to the Wedge.

The introduction of the Wedge meant the introduction of a whole new line of Campers.

refined and the body became more rigid. The front of the Wedge featured controlled deformation technology and a protective front frame to protect passengers in crashes. Doors were larger and were reinforced for side impacts. The sliding side door was also larger, which made getting people or cargo into a Bus a bit easier. There was a "break" in the body, a little above halfway up, to keep it from looking too boxy. The rear door was hinged at the top and sported a much larger window than the Bay Window. The engine was also refitted to be lower at the top, which added a good bit

of luggage space. Engine air intakes were of the same design as the Bay Window's, but were larger. Chrome highlights on the body hardware disappeared in favor of black hardware. One of the biggest improvements came in the form of better corrosion resistance, making rust less of an enemy.

The Wedge would come in the familiar forms of the Panelvan, the Kombi, the Microbus, the High-top Panelvan, the Single Cab Pickup, and the Double Cab Pickup. The new design allowed for more cargo capacity—people or product. Payload on the new vehicle

Above: The driver's area became much more contemporary in the Wedge. It was more comfortable, and the instrumentation gave the driver much more information.

Bottom: The interior of the Campers was becoming more and more refined. It still offered a bed, a kitchen, and a living room, but was a bit more spacious.

In the early 1980s, the Transporter got something it had never had—water. The air-cooled engine was finally abandoned in favor of water cooling. The Transporter would now have more power and better interior heating.

was quite high at almost 1,000 kilograms (2,205 pounds) and the new Kombi and Microbus versions were available in configurations that would seat up to nine passengers. Overall, the interior of the new Bus was much more refined when compared to the previous models. For the front passengers, the seats were redesigned and were more adjustable and comfortable. The dash more closely resembled contemporary design and was a far cry from the basic dashes of the early years. The larger body allowed a roomier and more open interior. One of the few interior items that did not improve was the heating system, which stayed the same (heat exchangers) and would not really improve until the introduction of the water-cooled engines.

Under the new body, the changes to the suspension were just as radical. With the new Bus the torsion bar suspension was gone. The Wedge would have a double wishbone front axle with coil springs, regular shock absorbers, and a sway bar. The rear suspension kept the independent trailing arm setup and would also use coil springs and shock absorbers. The change to the suspension was primarily an economic decision, as the new setup was cheaper to manufacture than the torsion bar suspension. It also freed up a bit of space, as it was no longer necessary to run the bars and their housings across the chassis. A rack-and-pinion steering system replaced the worm gear setup, greatly improving steering response.

What did stay the same for the Wedge was the power supply. The Volkswagen engineers decided to keep the engine in the back of the Bus, even though the new Volkswagen passenger cars had gone to a front engine, front-wheel drive setup. Both tradition and Volkswagen's belief that the rear was the best place for the engine drove this decision. Although the body and suspension were quite different from the previous models, the engine was much the same, and it was a problem. With the smaller engine, the 1,584-cc model, the Wedge was quite underpowered and had a top speed of only 68 miles per hour (110 kilometers per hour). Even with the largest available engine, the 1,970-cc model, the new Bus had very slow acceleration, taking about 18 seconds to reach 60 miles per hour, and could only achieve a top speed of around 79 miles per hour (127 kilometers per hour). This meant that the new and improved Bus was actually slower than the last Bay Window model. Power was driven to the wheels with either a four-speed manual gearbox or a three-speed

automatic. The fuel tank, which had a capacity of 13.2 gallons, was moved forward, which put the weight closer to the center of the vehicle. With an advertised fuel consumption of 21 miles per gallon, the air-cooled Wedge would have a theoretical range of 277 miles.

Members of the motoring press seemed to like the new Bus, especially in the areas of interior comfort, safety, and suspension, but they did notice the performance problem. In 1981, Volkswagen addressed the lack of power. The first more powerful engine offered was the four-cylinder diesel and, for the first time, a Bus would have a radiator. The little diesel had a displacement of 1.6 liters and produced 50 horsepower at 4,200 rpm. While the horsepower rating was about the same as the air-cooled engine, the inherent low-end torque of a diesel made the Bus much more drivable,

The Syncro, first offered in 1985, gave the more adventurous Transporter owner the benefit of four-wheel drive.

The Wedge influenced the design of its European siblings like this larger, front-engined, water-cooled van of the 1980s—here shown in four-wheel drive for all terrain rescues. The Wedge's character did not make the leap, however. *Volkswagen of America*

especially if loaded or towing a small trailer or boat. It was the same diesel offered in the Golf, and the engine fit nicely in the Wedge without major modifications. However, the engine was 200 pounds heavier than the air-cooled unit, which did affect the vehicle's weight bias. As fuel costs were soaring around the planet, a big benefit of the diesel was its ability to get almost 40 miles per gallon, or 538 miles per tankful, in a relatively large vehicle.

For those who just had to have a gas engine, some water-cooled solutions were on the way. The first to come was a 1.9-liter water-cooled flat four. In 1983, a 90-horsepower, fuel-injected engine was offered with optional power steering. Also in 1983, Volkswagen introduced the Caravelle, a modern Samba devoted to being a more comfortable people carrier. In 1985, a 110-horsepower gasoline-injected engine was offered, as well as a new turbo diesel. In the same year, the

Syncro, dubbed the "intelligent four-wheel drive," was introduced by Volkswagen. This system, which was available in the Golf as well as the Bus, greatly improved traction in slippery conditions and allowed for better off-road performance. Instead of an all-gear system, the Syncro used a viscous coupling to regulate the four-wheel drive.

By 1986, the six-millionth Bus was produced, making it the most successful vehicle of its type in history. More than half of the Buses being produced by this time were exported, but the increasingly competitive market was again dictating a change. The lifespan of designs was becoming shorter for the Bus. The Wedge was on its way out, and while it never attracted the cult following of the Split Window and the Bay Window, it was nonetheless a capable and popular vehicle. Often, the fond feelings loyalists had toward the earlier models never allowed them to judge the Wedge fairly and on its own merits. But those who scoff at the Wedge are quite shortsighted. Whether used for day-to-day use or for a drive across the country, there was no comparison between the later Wedges and its "bread-loaf-bodied" predecessors. When it came to performance and comfort, the Wedge would win in both categories.

In summary, the Wedge should not be criticized for lacking the personality of its predecessors; rather, its critics should recognize that the Wedge had its own personality—vibrant, colorful, and strong—but different.

A traveling maternity ward, complete with incubator. *Volkswagen of America*

The Wedge was also offered as a Pickup, although in America it did not have the impact of the previous models. *Volkswagen of America*

The impossible finally occurred in 1992, when Volkswagen introduced the fourth-generation Transporter. For decades Volkswagen engineers had praised the rear-engine configuration as a safer, better-handling design, but in 1992 the engine went to the front of the Bus. There were some distinct advantages to this arrangement. First, with the engine in the front, more mass was in front of the passengers, helping to protect them in head-on collisions. The second major benefit was more cargo space in the rear. Without the rear-engine compartment, the floor of the Bus could remain flat all the way to the rear door, a feature that most other vans already offered. This arrangement was very helpful to commercial customers, and especially those who chose the long wheelbase variant.

The length of the standard body was 186 inches (4,707 mm) with a wheelbase of 114 inches (2,920 mm), while the long-wheel base version was 199 inches (5,107 mm) long with a wheelbase of 129 inches (3,320 mm). The vehicle had a width of 63 inches (1,620 mm), a height of 55 inches (1,415 mm), and a 7-inch (180-mm) ground clearance. The new model would be the heaviest Bus, weighing in at 3,370 to 3,746 pounds (1,525 to 1,695 kilograms) for the regular version and 3,635 to 3,856 pounds (1,645 to 1,745 kilograms) for the long-wheelbase model. It would also be the most powerful; towing capacity was 1,547 pounds (700 kilograms) with a brakeless trailer. Initially it was available with a choice of three engines: a 2-liter gas model, a 2.5-liter gas model, or a 2.4-liter diesel model. The 2-liter (actually 1,968-cc) was a four-cylinder, and produced 80 horsepower at 4,300 rpm. The 2.5-liter (2,461-cc) model was a five-cylinder producing 115 horsepower at 4,500 rpm. Power was transferred to the wheels by either a five-speed manual or a four-speed automatic. The suspension was independent on all four wheels. On the front, the Bus returned to a torsion bar for spring, while the rear featured semi-trailing arms and coil springs. Disc brakes were used front and rear. The new Transporter was also available with the Syncro four-wheel drive option. The system still used a viscous coupling to distribute power, but off-road enthusiasts felt that the earlier Syncro had better off-pavement capabilities.

This newest Bus was as good as any vehicle in its class, but it meant an end to the Transporter's rear-

Below: To compete with the new generations of vans offered by virtually all of the automotive giants, Volkswagen introduced the EuroVan in 1992. *Volkswagen of America*

Next two pages: Camping was still a favorite pastime for Volkswagen owners. The later models could be bought in basic form or with a number of options. Here a tent fits conveniently to the rear door, giving the camper some privacy, including a stand-up shower stall.

Above: Models like the EuroVan "Weekender" continue to do what their predecessors did decades before. They offer a comfortable vehicle for daily transportation as well as a weekend getaway. With the many options available, the EuroVan can be quite comfortable when camping. It is a testament to the original designs that the basic theory of the vehicle has not changed in a half-century.

engined tradition. The new vehicle was much more akin to the other minivans on the road than the surviving Split Windows, Bay Windows, and Wedges.

Many began to wonder if the factory would ever return to its roots, and encouragement came in 1998. This was when the "New Beetle" hit the streets. Could the factory do the same with the Bus? Well, the news is encouraging.

At the present time, Volkswagen designers and engineers are working on a number of ideas, all of which connect to the roots of the original transporter. When the new one comes, expect a vehicle with retro looks and state-of-the-art engineering.

Even if the factory does succeed in producing as good a retro Bus as it did with the New Beetle, things will never be the same. Apart from the arching body,

Above: The New Beetle debuted in 1998. The bug's resurrection prompted many to wonder if the Volkswagen would do the same with the Transporter.

Next two pages: Volkswagen showed this concept for a new Transporter at the 2001 North American International Auto Show. *Volkswagen of America*

the New Beetle has little in common with the old, and it is safe to say that if Volkswagen did bring out a retro Bus, the differences would be as dramatic. The New Beetle was not the People's Car, and the New Bus will not be the "Bulli."

The world's love of the older Bus is a funny thing. It got away with less performance and comfort, yet became a legend. While the world zipped by in cars, the Bus chugged along like an old tugboat in a world of speedboats.

Even if you were always in a hurry, when you rode in a Bus you suddenly had all the time in the world, actually going slow enough to enjoy the scenery. Perhaps in some cases doctors should write prescriptions for Buses instead of antidepressants.

Pages 72–73: Like the New Beetle, the New Microbus is to be a modern vehicle that will have little in common with the original Transporter, other than shape. On this concept model, the front-mounted V-6 engine puts out more than 230 horsepower. *Volkswagen of America*

Below: The concept vehicle's interior is light-years beyond the original in both comfort and safety. *Volkswagen of America*

While the concept is the same, the technology has changed dramatically. The new vehicle offers television screens in the seat backrests to make the traveling hours pass a bit faster. A cockpit screen for the driver is linked to a camera in the back of the vehicle to assist in backing up. *Volkswagen of America*

Chapter 5

Community

Every group of automotive enthusiasts seems to have its own personality, which is often dictated by the personality of the vehicle. But they all pale in comparison to the Volkswagen folks.

When an individual buys a Bus or a Beetle, regardless of year or type, he or she enters two new worlds. The first world is that of the logical and user-friendly German engineering of their Volkswagen. If buyers have worked on other cars, they will almost instantly appreciate the logical, simple approach to the design and assembly of the vehicle. The second world they enter, if they so choose, is the Volkswagen community. People of the Bus community, along with their brothers and sisters in the Beetle community, are like no other. They are by far the friendliest group of people in the automotive world. They offer coffee. They share their camping area. They clean up the litter before they leave. They'll restore a vehicle, expending

Above: When the decision to buy has been made, take your time. Look at a number of Buses before buying. An emotional purchase can be satisfying in the short term, but it may cause headaches down the line.

great amounts of sweat and money—and then they'll take their wonderfully restored Split Window Camper on a 500-mile odyssey to the middle of the woods and camp in it. When traveling, they stop a lot. Coupled with the slow speeds of their vehicles, this makes for some leisurely journeys. While the rest of the world flies along hunched over the steering wheel with tight white knuckles, the Volkswagen community putters along laughing and talking. If a 300-mile trip takes eight hours, so be it.

Buying

For those interested obtaining a Bus and joining the community, there are a couple of ways to go. The first is to buy a well-restored Bus. By well-restored, I don't necessarily mean a perfect show winner, but nice enough to turn heads. This will be the quickest path to get on the road, but it has the highest initial cost.

The opposite extreme is the junkyard approach—find a derelict Bus in need of repair and drag it home. The downsides to this approach are formidable, but the benefits are the highest. The first benefit is

The price of admission into the Bus community is relatively inexpensive. In virtually every town in America, affordable Buses are for sale. With a little TLC they can be very trustworthy.

While much of the joy is in owning a great, historically significant vehicle, a great deal of pleasure can be gained by joining the Bus community. The Volkswagen community is a funny thing, with folks from every walk of life.

entry-level expense. Drag-home Buses are cheap and sometimes free. I know people who have paid no more than the service of getting it out of someone's backyard because they are tired of having to run the Weed Eater around it. If you buy parts wisely and supply your own labor, it is possible to have a nice Bus for a reasonable price. But beware—these projects can become money pits, especially if you overestimate your ability as a mechanic. If you end up breaking as many things as you fix and have to rely on a professional mechanic, you're better off buying a restored bus. But if you are willing to read and listen, there is no reason that a reasonably intelligent person cannot disassemble and reassemble a bus. The third choice lies somewhere in between the two previous examples. It is to buy a "driver" in need of attention. The term "driver" typically refers to a vintage car that sees regular road use. A driver in need of attention should be mechanically sound, but may have nasty carpet, faded paint, and rotten weather stripping. The trick is to find one that can be used while it is slowly being refreshed. This option allows for camping, a ride to work, and a weekend project. The price of a driver in need will fall somewhere between a junker and a restored model, depending on the condition.

Clubs and People

If you want to have your Bus and keep to yourself, that's fine. But if you want to meet others with the same interests, the Bus Club community is wonderful. Throughout the United States (and the world, for that matter), a thriving community of Volkswagen owners has organized into regional clubs. Regardless of where you live, chances are there is a club close by. Clubs usually meet once a month and schedule a number of events for members and visitors from other clubs.

Events range from cruises to campouts to car shows and swap meets. The best place to find clubs and club events is the Internet.

An example is the Full Moon Bus Club. Located in the North Carolina and Virginia area, the Full Moon Club schedules regular monthly camping trips during the full moon (When else?). Camping involves a full range of activities. Some purists sleep in the Buses. Others pitch enough tents to house a pharaoh's army. Kids are usually everywhere. Someone is always cooking something that smells really good, so you tend to stay hungry. Topics of conversation vary, but most center around technical Volkswagen matters.

Club shows are another nice way to spend a weekend. Nice cars are arranged for viewing and judging, while the perimeter is filled with drivers, vendors, and the general public. When attending these outings a person will meet a number of different types of Volkswagen owners. Members of the Volkswagen public will usually fall into six major categories:

The Purist. The holy grail of the Purist is originality. If it was not on the Bus when it left the factory, it should not be on the Bus now. Period. No exceptions.

Owning a Bus means more than working on an old vehicle. Once it's roadworthy, the box on wheels will provide miles of enjoyment. While many classic cars stay covered in garages, Buses tend to stay on the road.

For the industrious, restoring an old Bus can be an economical way to end up with a very nice vehicle—but beware. If you don't provide your own labor, a restoration project can become very expensive. If you have settled on a mechanic to do the work, before you buy, get a ballpark price on the restoration. But realize that until the job is finished, no one will know the exact cost. Often more problems are found as repairs are made.

If Purists were in charge of the government, it is quite possible that deviation from factory specs would result in seizure of the vehicle and the flogging of the owner.

The Authority. Authorities know everything and have done everything. They often act annoyed when asked a question, but don't be alarmed. If you did not ask, they would have no way to show how much they know, which is usually their favorite activity. Take their advice with a nod of the head and don't argue. Even with proof, you will never be right.

The Cheap Fixer. Members of this group usually include young, fresh-out-of-school owners with little money, or members with two or three hundred kids who take all of their money. Their world is filled with used parts and jury-rigged systems. Coat hangers hold up mufflers, and duct tape is a major structural element. The Cheap Fixers often have more spirit than any other group. Cheap Fixers learn quickly. They tend to ask questions, read manuals and, through self-reliance, learn a great deal about keeping the thing running. They are often the best roadside mechanics.

The Radical Changer. Radical Changers see the factory Bus as a starting place. While they love their Buses, they are constantly reengineering and modifying them. The Radical Changers have been responsible for Bus limousines, shortened Buses, lowered Buses, chopped Buses, four-wheel-drive Buses, and

There are still many Transporters out there that run and drive well but need a little care. This option allows both the economy of a lower price and the benefit of a vehicle that can be driven immediately and gradually restored.

The greatest enemy of the Bus is rust. Even extensive rust can be repaired, but it takes either a good bit of knowledge and skill or a good bit of money. Prospective buyers should always conduct a thorough rust inspection.

They are still out there. The tremendous production numbers mean that many Buses remain, waiting like a puppy for an owner. If a prospective project is relatively rust-free, check it out from front to back. Write down everything you see that needs fixing and replacing. Then check prices in catalogs, and add a bit for all of the things that you don't see.

As the years go by, there are fewer and fewer Buses to choose from, especially the Split Windows. Sometimes it is best to buy two beat-up Buses and make one good one.

Below: The more you look at a Bus before you buy, the better off you will be. Many buyers wait until after they buy to pull up carpets, and sometimes they get a nasty surprise. The seller of this Split Window has already lifted the carpets to show the rust-free condition of the floor.

Some old Buses are probably too far gone, but each deserves a close inspection. Sadly, this old Split Window Camper has probably seen its last trip, but who knows? Maybe someone with more time than sense will take a shot at it.

even electric Buses. They are likely to pour massive amounts of time and money into a vehicle with little hope of ever getting it out. Volkswagen has provided the world with two of the most customizable vehicles in the history of the automobile. The Beetle and the Bus offer the average buyer a chance to personalize his or her ride at a very reasonable cost. Bus customizing could be taken in many different directions. The vehicle could be simply modified for business purposes.

This may consist of little more than a few bars mounted by a dry cleaner to turn a Bus into a delivery van. Interiors can be modified to haul all types of cargo or, more often, people. Of course, the most memorable are the "hippie" rigs, decked out for a wild life on the road. The large body had plenty of room for extreme peace, which promoted understanding and had the added bonus of making the police want to search the vehicle.

Advice is usually an abundant commodity within the Volkswagen community. With wisdom from endless manuals and thousands of shade-tree mechanics, there is no part of a Bus that can't be healed.

On the next two pages: One of the biggest benefits of owning a Bus comes from the entry into a Bus club. Groups like the Full Moon Bus Club are made up of perhaps the friendliest people of any automotive group. When you go to a show or camping meet, even if you don't know anyone there, you will not meet a stranger.

Some go all the way after buying their Buses, and when they're finished, the only thing stock is the sheet metal in the body. *Kathy Jacobs*

The Automotive Perfectionist. These people can be into either originality or change, but their goal is automotive perfection. They will wash the paint off of a vehicle. They clean, detail, buff, repaint, and shine. They clean the treads of their tires. They make sure their brake lines are polished. Some Perfectionists even lose at car shows because their car is more perfect than anything the factory ever produced.

The Clueless. They are usually well-meaning, but they are the kind of folk who should not be allowed to change a lightbulb on their own. They have an engine that is always one stroke away from seizing, or their brake shoes are grinding away drums and rotors. They are always worried about things that don't really matter. They have a $4,000 paint job, and don't change the oil.

Also remember, club members can be more than one type. You can have a Purist Authority or a Cheap Fixer Authority. A Modifier Perfectionist or a Cheap Fixer Modifier. Every club usually has a menagerie of these types of Bus owners and the result is a steady stream of gossip and commentary. The Purists are writhing in pain over a Radical Changer's plan to lower his 1965 Samba, paint it hot pink, and install a waterbed. The Changers are mad because the Purists will let old Buses rot in the backyard before they will sell them to a Radical Changer. The Perfectionists are usually off in a world of their own, polishing a brake pedal. The Cheap Fixers are roving around asking questions and being perpetually disappointed with the Purists for only advising to buy the proper part and install it properly. They try not to ask the Radical Changers, because a simple ques-

continued on page 92

Above: For some, the greatest pleasure is keeping their Bus as close to the stock look as possible.

Left: This vehicle is straight, and it also has a number of personal refinements. It's in good running order, and the owner claims 236,000 miles with no engine rebuild. Note the handmade cargo carrier over the cab, the ski boat ladder stored on the side, and the homemade tent.

Next four pages: There aren't a lot of vehicles that can be painted with a brush and look good. Perhaps the Bus is the only one that can carry it off. Whether it is a paisley paint job or a Muppet jungle, the Bus looks good wearing it.

SALEM IMPORT SERVICE

SALEM, VA
540-389-8587

THIS MAY BE AN
UGLY BUS BUT
I L♥VE IT!

PRODUCT OF THE
70's

THIS IS YOUR BRAIN.

THIS IS YOUR
BRAIN ON DRUGS.

One of the greatest assets shared by Volkswagen owners is their ability to poke fun at themselves. Whether it is a bumper sticker that says "Honk if parts fall off," or a sticker poking fun at their Transporter's slow speed, typical Bus owners don't take themselves too seriously—a rare and welcome trait in today's world.

continued from page 86

tion about a carburetor adjustment will yield an hour of pondering and a proposal for fuel injection, turbochargers, and nitrous oxide.

But it all comes together nicely. I have never been to a Volkswagen Beetle or Bus show, meet, or campout where I did not meet someone new, nice, and interesting. We spend more time in our world interacting through computers, cell phones, and televisions and not enough time sitting on the front porch talking. Buses not only keep alive old automotive technology. They are the seeds that grow the clubs, which give bloom to events. These events are places where strangers meet. People who have never met spend hours talking to each other about their common love, Buses. But they also talk

In an era of proliferating cell phones, televisions, and video games, there is no doubt that every American family could benefit from owning a Bus. A few weekends a year with a campfire and a Coleman lantern will provide memories that children will always enjoy.

about everything else. They are a throwback to simpler times. Next time you drive by and see the friendly face of a Split Window or a Bay, still smiling even though it has been cast into the weeds to rust, you should stop and ask, "How much?" In a year or so you might be sitting by a fire in the mountains with your trusty Bus behind you, reflecting on how you impressed the wife and kids with that roadside repair. Through effort and appreciation, you can build a bond with an old Bus that would be.

The Front Cover Shot: Who could have guessed that the little German Bus was would become so popular in America and around the world, and would become so closely associated with the hippie lifestyle of the 1960s and 1970s?

Index

Assembly line, 12
Bus Clubs, 76–79, 82, 86, 92, 94
Buying tips, 74, 76, 78, 80, 81
Custom tent, 51, 64, 65
Engine
    1,131 cc, 20
    1,192 cc, 31
    1,500 cc, 36
    1,584 cc, 43, 59
    1,600 cc, 45
    1,700 cc, 45, 46
    1,800 cc, 46
    1,968 cc, 62
    1,970 cc, 59
Ford, Henry, 9
Full Moon Bus Club, 77, 83
Goering, Hermann, 14
Guthrie, Arlo, 52
Haesner, Alfred, 17
History of Volkswagen, 8–19
Hitler, Adolf, 8, 9
Nordhoff, Heinz, 7, 17, 18, 44
Pon, Ben, 17, 20
Porsche, Dr. Ferdinand, 12, 14
Production numbers
    1950, 23
    1951, 28
    1952, 30
    1953, 31, 32
    1957, 35
    1962, 36
    1965, 36
    1968, 44, 45
    1970, 45
    1972, 51
    1977, 51
    1978, 51
Specifications
    1950, 20–22
    1953, 30, 31
    1963, 36

    1968, 42–44
    1974, 46, 51
    1980, 59–61
    1992, 62
Stocken (Hanover) factory, 33
Volkswagen Models and Variations
    Ambulance, 30, 45
    Bay Window (Type 2), 38–54
    Beetle, 6, 8, 14
    Camper, 32, 33, 46, 56, 57
    Campmobile, 48–50
    Caravelle, 60
    Crewcab, 35
    Double Cab Pickup, 31, 44, 45, 51, 56
    EuroVan, 63
    EuroVan Weekender, 66
    Golf, 54, 60, 61
    High-top Panelvan, 56
    Kombi, 17, 18, 23, 28, 30, 31, 35, 44, 45, 56, 58
    Kubelwagen, 10, 16
    Microbus Deluxe, 23, 36, 44
    Microbus, 17, 18, 23, 26, 28, 30, 31, 35, 44, 51, 52, 56, 58
    New Beetle, 67, 70
    New Microbus, 72, 73
    Panelvan, 16–18, 20, 21, 28, 29, 31, 32, 35, 44, 56
    People's Car, 9, 12
    Pickup, 26, 27, 30, 31, 35, 51, 62
    Rabbit, 54
    Samba, 18, 23, 26, 28–31, 35, 60
    Schwimmwagen, 11
    Scirocco, 54
    Single Cab Pickup, 44, 51, 56
    Split Window, 20–38
    Syncro, 59, 60, 61, 63
    Thing, 16
    Transporter concept, 68–71
    Wedge, 54–73
Westfalia, 34
Wolfsburg plant, 8, 14, 16, 17
World War II, 7, 14

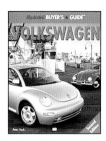
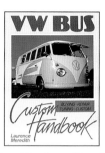

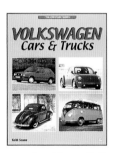

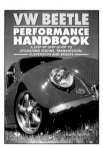
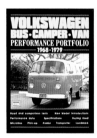